Our Death, Burial, and Resurrection in Christ

By Michael D Brown

Dedication

To God be the glory

Rom 6:6
Knowing this, that our old man is crucified with him, that the body of sin might be destroyed, that henceforth we should not serve sin.

Rom 6:4
Therefore we are buried with him by baptism into death: that like as Christ was raised up from the dead by the glory of the Father, even so we also should walk in newness of life.

Col 2:12
Buried with him in baptism, wherein also ye are risen with him through the faith of the operation of God, who hath raised him from the dead.

Gal:2:20
20 I am crucified with Christ: nevertheless I live; yet not I, but Christ liveth in me: and the life which I now live in the flesh I live by the faith of the Son of God, who loved me, and gave himself for me.

Our discussion examines these four verses and the three events outlined in these verses, namely Death, burial, and resurrection. We understand the universal testimony of scripture regarding death, that it is returning to dust:

Gen 3:19
In the sweat of thy face shalt thou eat bread, till thou return unto the ground; **for out of it wast thou taken:** for dust thou art, and unto dust shalt thou return.

We understand the euphemism, 'sleep' used throughout the bible especially in the Law and the Prophets as illustrated below:

1 Kgs 2:10
So David slept with his fathers, and was buried in the city of David.

1 Kgs 11:21
And when Hadad heard in Egypt that David slept with his fathers, and that Joab the captain of the host was dead, Hadad said to Pharaoh, Let me depart, that I may go to mine own country.

1 Kgs 11:43
And Solomon slept with his fathers,
and was buried in the city of David
his father: and Rehoboam his son
reigned in his stead.

1 Kgs 14:20
And the days which Jeroboam reigned
were two and twenty years: and he
slept with his fathers, and Nadab his
son reigned in his stead.

1 Kgs 14:31
And Rehoboam slept with his fathers,
and was buried with his fathers in
the city of David. And his mother's
name was Naamah an Ammonitess. And
Abijam his son reigned in his stead.

1 Kgs 15:8
And Abijam slept with his fathers;
and they buried him in the city of
David: and Asa his son reigned in his
stead.

1 Kgs 15:24
And Asa slept with his fathers, and
was buried with his fathers in the
city of David his father: and

Jehoshaphat his son reigned in his stead.

1 Kgs 16:6
So Baasha slept with his fathers, and was buried in Tirzah: and Elah his son reigned in his stead.

1 Kgs 16:28
So Omri slept with his fathers, and was buried in Samaria: and Ahab his son reigned in his stead.

1 Kgs 22:40
So Ahab slept with his fathers; and Ahaziah his son reigned in his stead.

1 Kgs 22:50
And Jehoshaphat slept with his fathers, and was buried with his fathers in the city of David his father: and Jehoram his son reigned in his stead.

2 Kgs 8:24
And Joram slept with his fathers, and was buried with his fathers in the city of David: and Ahaziah his son reigned in his stead.

2 Kgs 10:35
And Jehu slept with his fathers: and
they buried him in Samaria. And
Jehoahaz his son reigned in his
stead.

2 Kgs 13:9
And Jehoahaz slept with his fathers;
and they buried him in Samaria: and
Joash his son reigned in his stead.

2 Kgs 13:13
And Joash slept with his fathers; and
Jeroboam sat upon his throne: and
Joash was buried in Samaria with the
kings of Israel.

2 Kgs 14:16
And Jehoash slept with his fathers,
and was buried in Samaria with the
kings of Israel; and Jeroboam his son
reigned in his stead.

2 Kgs 14:22
He built Elath, and restored it to
Judah, after that the king slept with
his fathers.

2 Kgs 14:29
And Jeroboam slept with his fathers,
even with the kings of Israel; and
Zachariah his son reigned in his
stead.

2 Kgs 15:7
So Azariah slept with his fathers;
and they buried him with his fathers
in the city of David: and Jotham his
son reigned in his stead.

2 Kgs 15:22
And Menahem slept with his fathers;
and Pekahiah his son reigned in his
stead.

2 Kgs 15:38
And Jotham slept with his fathers,
and was buried with his fathers in
the city of David his father: and
Ahaz his son reigned in his stead.

2 Kgs 16:20
And Ahaz slept with his fathers, and
was buried with his fathers in the
city of David: and Hezekiah his son
reigned in his stead.

2 Kgs 20:21
And Hezekiah slept with his fathers:
and Manasseh his son reigned in his
stead.

2 Kgs 21:18
And Manasseh slept with his fathers,
and was buried in the garden of his
own house, in the garden of Uzza: and
Amon his son reigned in his stead.

2 Kgs 24:6
So Jehoiakim slept with his fathers:
and Jehoiachin his son reigned in his
stead.

2 Chron 9:31
And Solomon slept with his fathers,
and he was buried in the city of
David his father: and Rehoboam his
son reigned in his stead.

2 Chron 12:16
And Rehoboam slept with his fathers,
and was buried in the city of David:
and Abijah his son reigned in his
stead.

2 Chron 14:1
So Abijah slept with his fathers, and they buried him in the city of David: and Asa his son reigned in his stead. In his days the land was quiet ten years.

2 Chron 16:13
And Asa slept with his fathers, and died in the one and fortieth year of his reign.

2 Chron 21:1
Now Jehoshaphat slept with his fathers, and was buried with his fathers in the city of David. And Jehoram his son reigned in his stead.

2 Chron 26:2
He built Eloth, and restored it to Judah, after that the king slept with his fathers.

2 Chron 26:23
So Uzziah slept with his fathers, and they buried him with his fathers in the field of the burial which belonged to the kings; for they said,

He is a leper: and Jotham his son reigned in his stead.

2 Chron 27:9
And Jotham slept with his fathers, and they buried him in the city of David: and Ahaz his son reigned in his stead.

2 Chron 28:27
And Ahaz slept with his fathers, and they buried him in the city, even in Jerusalem: but they brought him not into the sepulchres of the kings of Israel: and Hezekiah his son reigned in his stead.

2 Chron 32:33
And Hezekiah slept with his fathers, and they buried him in the chiefest of the sepulchres of the sons of David: and all Judah and the inhabitants of Jerusalem did him honour at his death. And Manasseh his son reigned in his stead.

2 Chron 33:20
So Manasseh slept with his fathers, and they buried him in his own house:

and Amon his son reigned in his
stead.

Psa 13:3
Consider and hear me, O LORD my God:
lighten mine eyes, lest I sleep the
sleep of death;

Psa 78:50
He made a way to his anger; he spared
not their soul from death, but gave
their life over to the pestilence;

Psa 89:48
What man is he that liveth, and shall
not see death? shall he deliver his
soul from the hand of the grave?
Selah.

Isa 53:12
Therefore will I divide him a portion
with the great, and he shall divide
the spoil with the strong; because he
hath poured out his soul unto death:
and he was numbered with the
transgressors; and he bare the sin of
many, and made intercession for the
transgressors.

Eccles 9:5
**For the living know that they shall
die: but the dead know not any thing,
neither have they any more a reward;
for the memory of them is forgotten.**

We understand that when God breathed
the breath of life into man, Adam
became a *living soul, a living being.*
Soul is not something we have but it
is what we are. The last Adam, the
Lord Jesus Christ, became a
quickening spirit.

1 Cor 15:45
**And so it is written, The first man
Adam was made a living soul; the last
Adam was made a quickening spirit.**

Many argue against scripture and
stand in agreement with the serpent
[Satan] who said to Eve, "thou shalt
not surely die"

Gen 3:4
**And the serpent said unto the woman,
Ye shall not surely die:**

The traditional view of death places mankind at death in heaven, or hell, or in some other place like purgatory or Abraham's bosom. Some quote Luke 16 where the Lord Jesus mentions Abraham's bosom in the story he tells of the rich man and Lazarus. However, many fail to recognize that Christ uses the reference of Abraham's bosom from the Talmud, and he refutes their teaching in doing so, redirecting them to listen to Moses and the prophets which the religious leaders refused to do. The point of the story is to expose the false teachings of the religious leaders and to confirm the truth concerning death and resurrection as delineated in the law and the prophets. Note the following references where Abraham's bosom is found in the writings of the Jews long before Christ tells this story in Luke 16. Note examples from the Talmud:

1. Kiddushim (Treatise on Betrothal) fol. 72
2. Midrash Echah, fol 68.1
3. Midrash on Ruth, fol. 44, 2

4.   Midrash on Coheleth (Ecclesiastes) fol.86, 4
5.   Berachoth, fol. 18, 2- Treatise on Blessings

Anyone familiar with the Talmud and the teachings of the Jewish leaders of that day will quickly realize that the Lord Jesus Christ is refuting their false teaching. The idea that the dead are alive in death [an oxymoron] is very comforting to the masses and in part explains why so many embrace this view which contradicts the bible.

Prov 30:4
Who hath ascended up into heaven, or descended? who hath gathered the wind in his fists? who hath bound the waters in a garment? who hath established all the ends of the earth? what is his name, and what is his son's name, if thou canst tell?

John 3:13
And no man hath ascended up to heaven, **but he that came down from**

heaven, even the Son of man which is
in heaven.

The universal testimony of scripture
regarding death is clear and in
perfect harmony with all of the
writers of scripture without a hint
of disagreement. The exceptions to
death are few namely, the rapture
mentioned for Israel in 1 Corinthians
15 and in 1 Thessalonians
And also the separate and unique
rapture for the Body of Christ in
Col. 3:4

1 Cor 15:51
Behold, I shew you a mystery; We
shall not all sleep, but we shall all
be changed,

1 Thess 4:16
For the Lord himself shall descend
from heaven with a shout, with the
voice of the archangel, and with the
trump of God: and the dead in Christ
shall rise first:

These first two verses reference the
faithful remnant of Jews and Gentile

believers after the Body of Christ has been removed at Christ's earlier Appearing.

Col 3:4
When Christ, who is our life, shall appear, then shall ye also appear with him in glory.

This pretribulation rapture mentioned in Col. 3:4 belongs to the Body of Christ which cannot be a party to the tribulation where the worship of the Beast, false prophet, and Antichrist will reign. The Body of Christ will not be present when the mark of the Beast [666] is presented to the nations. No member of the Body of Christ can ever lose their eternal salvation, nor are we told that we must endure until the end [Christ's return] to be saved. Israel must endure until the end in order to be saved in the day when Christ returns.

Matt 10:22
And ye shall be hated of all men for
my name's sake: but he that endureth
to the end shall be saved.

Right division of scripture is
imperative if we are to understand
what God has intended for us and the
key to correctly dividing is given in
2 Tim 2:15

2 Tim 2:15
Study to shew thyself approved unto
God, a workman that needeth not to be
ashamed, rightly dividing the word of
truth.

Eph 2:13
13 But now in Christ Jesus ye who
sometimes were far off are made nigh
by the blood of Christ.

2 Wherein in time past ye walked
according to the course of this world,
according to the prince of the power of
the air, the spirit that now worketh in
the children of disobedience:

7 That in the ages to come he might
shew the exceeding riches of his

grace in his kindness toward us through Christ Jesus.

Above we note Paul's threefold division of God's dealings with man, and it is, *times past, but now, and the ages to come.*
Additionally, we must recognize the things that differ like Law and grace, and the program for the nation Israel and the separate and distinct program for the Body of Christ. We must see Paul's letters and to whom he is addressing at every turn. Sometimes he speaks to the Little Flock, the faithful remnant and sometimes he speaks to the Body of Christ. Sometimes there are parallel truths that apply to both, for example death passing onto all men, with the rapture(s) for each group differing in their execution and purpose.
Our main purpose is to examine the resurrection of the Body of Christ, noting parallels with that of Israel. We have thus far spoken mostly of

death because it is a universal experience.

Rom 5:12
Wherefore, as by one man sin entered into the world, and death by sin; and so death passed upon all men, **for that all have sinned:**

Here we pause to quickly cover some common objections before we discuss in detail our main purpose. Some point to the malefactor who died next to Christ and they suggest that Christ took him to paradise that very day in which they both died. The bible however, teaches that Christ was dead for 3 days and to suggest otherwise is to disagree with the gospel that saves and to invalidate Christ's own words where he himself stated that he would rise from death on that 3rd day

John 2:19
Jesus answered and said unto them, Destroy this temple, and in three days I will raise it up.

The malefactor asked to be remembered when Christ entered His earthly kingdom, and Christ promised Him entrance into that Theocratic Davidic Kingdom which will one day be set up on earth at Christ's 2nd coming. Some point to Elijah and Enoch and suggest that they ascended into heaven and Christ says that no one has yet ascended into the heavens. This includes Moses and Elijah, as the mount of transfiguration was a preview of coming attractions. Lastly, Paul was stoned and left for dead, and he saw a vision of heaven as he was caught away **[not caught up, the greek word is harpagenta, meaning having been caught away]   Verb/ Acc/sing/masc/part/aor/pass]** No one without a resurrection body can enter heaven and even Christ had one before he ascended. In our current status we are mortal and this we must put off. We are in corrupted sinful bodies defiled by our old sinful nature. True our sins are paid for and we are complete in Him, but we do not carry our ability to sin with us to heaven in our mortality. We discover the passage in 1 Corinthians 15:12-58 on resurrection directed at those living and dead believers at Christ's 2nd coming [the Parousia] Appears with parallel truth for the Body of Christ. We will also require a resurrection body suited for our new environment, as we formerly bore the image of the earthly, we will bear the image of the heavenly.

48 As is the earthy, such are they also that are earthy: and as is the heavenly, such are they also that are heavenly.

49 And as we have borne the image of the earthy, we shall also bear the image of the heavenly.

50 Now this I say, brethren, that flesh and blood cannot inherit the kingdom of God; neither doth corruption inherit incorruption.

We have retroactive positional truth because we are said to have died with

Christ; we are crucified with him; we are buried in baptism with him, and that is the one baptism that applies to the Body of Christ mentioned in Eph 4. The baptism of the Holy Spirit that identifies us with Christ in his death, burial, and resurrection.

Members of the body of Christ do experience death and like all men of all ages, fall asleep in death. There is no life again without resurrection, and the resurrection to life again always requires a body. There is no disembodied life for us and there is no example of it anywhere in the bible.

James 2:26
For as the body without the spirit is dead, so faith without works is dead also.

James makes the issue clear that without the spirit [breath of life] there is no living soul.
So, when Christ who is our life appears, we will appear with Him in glory.

4 When Christ, who is our life, shall appear, then shall ye also appear with him in glory.

We will be removed from this life without any notice, as there are no signs or wonders, or any way to predict exactly when this will occur. We are given only this tiny bit of information, but is it enough in light of all the rest of scripture that must occur after this happens and we are absent from any mention in the remainder of the Word of God. We are absent from Hebrews (addressed to Hebrews) through to Revelation. The focus returns to the Kingdom that will be ushered in following the tribulation. The focus returns to God's chosen people Israel and to the promises that God has yet to fulfill.

The members of the body of Christ who died before the APPEARING of Christ will be raised from sleep and they along with the living members of the body will appear with Christ in glory.

9 And when he had opened the fifth seal, I saw under the altar the souls of them that were slain for the word of God, and for the testimony which they held:

10 And they cried with a loud voice, saying, How long, O Lord, holy and true, dost thou not judge and avenge our blood on them that dwell on the earth?

11 And white robes were given unto every one of them; and it was said unto them, that they should rest yet for a little season, until their fellowservants also and their brethren, that should be killed as they were, should be fulfilled.

Rev 20:5
~~**finished This thousand years first**~~

These verses explain themselves very well. The dead were not speaking as the dead can not speak, yet like righteous Abel's blood crying out

from the ground; the cry for Justice
is herein addressed and through
symbolism the Justice of God
addresses the issue, and he tells the
dead to continue resting [sleeping]
until their fellow servants join them
in death and the time for God's wrath
takes place.
Concerning our own resurrection:

Rom 6:5
**For if we have been planted together
in the likeness of his death, we
shall be also in the likeness of his
resurrection:**

1 Cor 15:21
**For since by man came death, by man
came also the resurrection of the
dead.**

This last verse speaks again of a
parallel truth for both the Body of
Christ and saved Israel in the
future. Since death came by man and
it has passed upon all men, so too
the resurrection also came by man
[Christ] and this is the return to
life.

Romans 6:5 confirms that we who have been planted together in the likeness of his death [We share in his death -retroactive positional truth] We will share in the likeness of his resurrection. The use of 'likeness' signals the figure **simile** and draws our attention to a comparison; namely that our resurrection will mirror Christ's in some form or fashion. Because we will appear in glory with Him when He appears. This 'appearing' does not negate the necessity of resurrection and all that it entails: the shedding of corruption and mortality, and being outfitted for the eternal state with the appropriate body, the likeness of which will resemble Christ's body. We are guaranteed to be conformed to the image of the son:

Rom 8:29
For whom he did foreknow, he also did predestinate to be conformed to the image of his Son, **that he might be the firstborn among many brethren.**

When we are removed and we appear
with Christ in glory, we will have
been conformed to the image of the
Son, and we will share in His
likeness, His image, and we will most
certainly have shed our vile bodies
which we now occupy as unwilling
tenants. We have a death when we
believe in Christ's death, burial,
and resurrection. We are buried with
him and our lives are hidden in
Christ.

**Col 3:3 For ye are dead, and your
life is hid with Christ in God.**

We are dead to sin, and alive to God
through Jesus Christ our Lord. We now
have victory over the old sin nature,
which previously reigned over us. We
live in, through and by means of
Christ who lives in us as He has
raised us with Him and we are seated
in Him in heavenly places.

**Eph 2:6
And hath raised us up together, and
made us sit together in heavenly
places in Christ Jesus:**

Our resurrection with regard to what has already occurred is spoken of in the past tense and the future reality of it is also in view as we are yet to possess it, yet to shed our flesh and blood bodies, yet to inherit eternal life discarding mortality, yet to take hold of incorruption casting aside corruption.

The fact of our burial with Christ makes us following crucifixion dead to sin; dead to the law, dead to ordinances; and buried in death makes us detached from the fleshly carnal appetites that once were our propensity. We are buried and oblivious to the old things which have passed away. We are new creations [not born again] and entirely new spiritual species IN CHRIST, in the Body of Christ we are no longer what we used to be, no longer slaves, and enslaved, and no longer earthly minded. We now possess the mind of Christ, and we seek those things which are above. Our removal [rapture] is also a mystery, a sacred secret only mentioned once in the

Bible. This is a revealed secret and yet very little is said, and this is also true of the Body of Christ itself, a sacred secret, now revealed. Our death, burial, and resurrection is tied and inextricably bound to Christ as we are the members of his Body and we will share all spiritual blessings in the heavenlies; we are heirs and joint heirs with Christ. It is my prayer that this short book helps you to see what is the fellowship of the mystery Paul speaks of in Eph 3:9. The gospel that saves us is 1 Cor. 15:1-4. Simply believe in Christ's death on the cross according to the scripture as payment in full for our sins. Christ's burial [he was actually dead - his humanity] and Christ's resurrection on the 3rd day. Believe the gospel and you will be eternally saved instantly.